Roped In

Creative Craft Projects Made With Rope
(and Other Awesome Things)

Gemma Patford

Roped In

Creative Craft Projects Made With Rope
(and Other Awesome Things)

Gemma Patford

hardie grant books

Contents

Little Friends p.092

Furry Friends p.110

Let's Celebrate! p.128

Hello! I wonder if you are reading this from the comfort of your lounge or bedroom, or quietly hiding from your children in the bathroom. Wherever you are, I can tell already we are going to get along. How do I know this? Well, firstly, you've picked up this book, which says to me that: 1. You're crafty; 2. You want help colour-coding your bookshelf; or 3. Both! Whichever reason it is, you are my people.

First thing's first. THANK YOU FOR BUYING MY BOOK! Or, if you are loitering in the bookstore flipping through these pages, thank you for thinking about buying my book ... But know that you're loitering – you should probably go and buy it.

My name is Gemma: I'm a self-taught jack of all trades, master of some and the occasional baker of overworked, hard muffins. Everyone in my family is creative. When I was growing up, Dad ran his own painting and decorating business from home; my mother is a great illustrator and knitter, and speaks muddled French; my sister sews

like a demon; and my brother can make pretty much anything out of wood. My family would always say, 'Give Gemma a roll of masking tape and she'll be quiet for hours.'

My grandmother (on my dad's side) was an avid thrift shopper. She volunteered every week at her local charity shop and would always bring home spectacular (and sometimes not so spectacular) vintage items. I loved her home. It was full of pre-loved items, which she breathed new life into.

So, fast-forward through my happy childhood to university.

I completed a Bachelor of Science. Weird, I know. Don't let that throw you. It's OK. I've forgotten everything! Science whaaaa?? After that, I decided to enrol in fashion school and have never looked back.

So, bringing you up to date, my muddled background has enabled me to collaborate with some of the industry's most awesome creatives both in Australia and overseas. Rope is my main thing, but it's not my only thing. It all started when I was given a beautiful handmade crochet basket from a friend. You shoulda seen this thing: it was beautiful, and I was totally inspired to make my own! My friend Mie, a seasoned maker, attempted to teach me how to crochet. I was terrible – I couldn't do it. I lasted two, three stitches before I lost interest. For those crochet experts out there, my hat goes off to you. You win, OK?!

From this crochet setback, I started searching for basket-making techniques that spoke to me (aka basket-making methods that were easier). I stumbled across a YouTube tutorial showing women in the United States wrapping vintage fabric around rope and coiling it together using a domestic sewing machine.

Something inside of me stirred. I HAD A DOMESTIC SEWING MACHINE, AND I HAD ROPE! I pulled out my trusty watercolour paints, decorated some cotton rope and crafted together my first-ever rope basket. I posted my new treasure on Instagram and the likes flooded in.

You might find yourself asking, 'What makes Gemma the authority on crafty things both rope and not?' Well, I am not the authority, but I am exceptionally good at LIFE ILLUSIONS. Making simple things LOOK fancy. Your friends will drop to their knees and ask, 'How do you do it? Where do you find the time?' and you'll flick your wrist like it's no big thaaaang, swish your hair around and casually laugh like a Hollywood A-lister being quizzed about their on-screen chemistry with their beautiful co-star.

Life illusion number one: my husband and I live in a tiny two-bedroom apartment, but we make it work. We host fun dinner parties, yet we have no dining table. We share our home with a fat, grumpy cat and an ever-growing toddler ... speaking of, I don't recall signing up for a toddler. I wanted a baby! My toddler refuses to leave the park graciously and is constantly

covered in jam. WE DON'T HAVE JAM IN THE HOUSE! OK, I've gone off script ...

Follow me – let me guide you past the smoke and mirrors of fabulous crafting. Together we will create the many projects featured in this book, most made with rope and others not, but all will convince your friends you have your life together.

You, my friend, have just been roped in by Gemma Patford.

Useful Things to Know

Before we get our hands dirty (and everything else), here are some basic knots and sewing techniques that you just gotta learn! I will be referring to these guys often, so to make it easier on you and to hit the ground running, find some time to learn these knots.

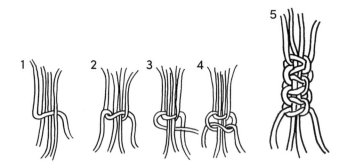

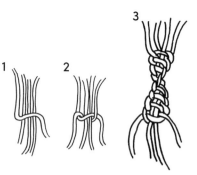

Square Knot

Step 1

Take four strands of rope. Take the first strand of rope on the left, bring it over the two middle strands and thread it under the last strand. It should resemble the number 4.

Step 2

Take the furthermost right strand, bring it under the two middle strands and thread it over the first strand.

Step 3

Take the first strand of rope on the left, bring it under the two middle strands, and thread it over the last strand.

Step 4

Take the furthermost right strand, bring it over the two middle strands and thread it over the first strand. It should resemble a reverse number 4.

Step 5

Pull the strands of rope tight and you have the finished square knot.

Half Knot Sinnet

Step 1

Take four strands of rope. Take the first strand of rope on the left, bring it over the two middle strands, and thread it under the last strand. It should resemble the number 4.

Step 2

Take the furthermost right strand, bring it under the two middle strands and thread it over the first strand.

Step 3

Repeat, repeat, repeat. The knots will slowly form a beautiful spiral.

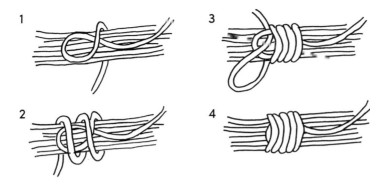

✧✧

Gathering Wrap

Step 1

Take a piece of rope and make a 'U' shape over the strands of rope you would like to 'gather'. Keep one end much longer than the other, and tuck this end under the strands of rope.

Step 2

Starting from the top of the 'U', take the longer end of the rope, and begin to wrap it around and around the 'U' and the strands you would like to gather.

Step 3

Once you reach the base of the 'U', thread the end of the rope through the loop.

Take the shorter strand of rope and pull tightly. You will see the loop being pulled inside the wrap.

Step 4

Trim any unsightly rope from the knot.

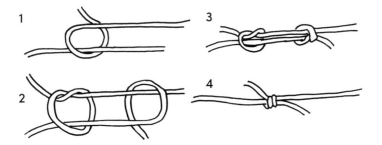

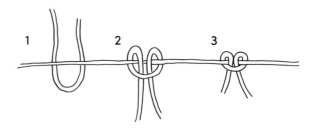

Fisherman's Knot

Step 1

Lay two strands of rope flat, with one sitting slightly above the other.

Step 2

Take the left strand of rope and bring it over the right strand, then under and through itself.

Step 3

Take the right strand of rope and bring it over the left strand, then under and through itself. Pull firmly.

Step 4

Pull the ends of the rope firmly until both knots tug and meet in the middle.

Lark Head Knot

Step 1

Take a strand of rope and fold it in half.

Step 2

Place a piece of wooden dowel or rope horizontally over the looped rope. This will be what the lark head knot will hang from.

Step 3

Fold the ends of the rope over the horizontal dowel or rope, and thread them through the loop.

Step 4

Pull firmly.

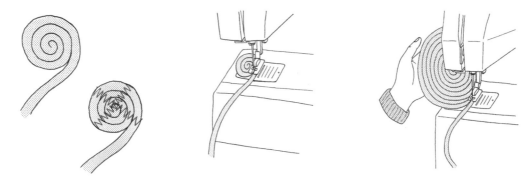

Sewing a Rope Coil

Step 1

Take your length of rope and coil it into a small circle, so it resembles a number 9.

Step 2

Zigzag stitch through the middle of the circle, from one side of the coil to the other, to bind the rope together, reversing over your stitches a few times to secure the coil in place. Repeat in the diagonal direction to the first line of stitching.

Step 3

Continue to add to the size of the rope coil by sewing the loose rope to the coil. Be sure that the zigzag stitch captures both the loose rope and the coil as you go.

Step 4

Sew the rope around the coil until you reach your desired width. This will be the base of your vessel.

Step 5

Lift the base at an angle against the left side of the machine. Continue to sew the rope together, which will create the vessel's sides and increase its height.

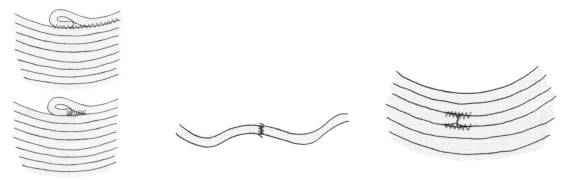

Step 6

When your vessel is your desired height, loop the last of piece of rope underneath itself to create a neat finish. Stitch the loop closed by reversing over this section a few times.

Step 7

Hold the loop up to the light. If there is a small gap, zigzag stitch over this a few times to close it up.

Step 8

If you run out of rope too soon, add another length of rope by stitching the two together with a zigzag stitch.

If a gap appears in the basket, zigzag stitch over it to create a web effect that covers the hole.

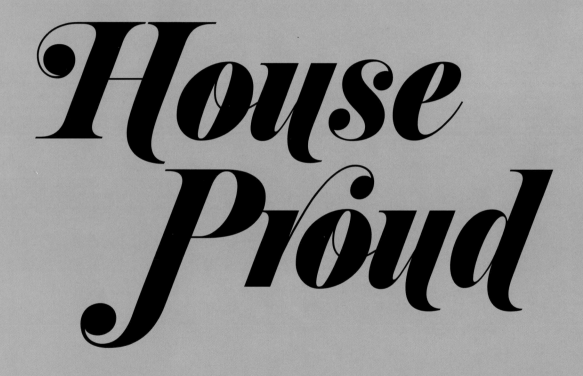

Make It Your Own

I am extremely preoccupied with my home's appearance. It may not look that way because of my cool-as-a-cucumber attitude (LOL), but it's no mistake that the spine of this book is one solid colour. That is so it will slide smoothly into the blue section of my colour-coded bookshelf.

I think the older I get the more homely I become. Our home is tiny: a two-bedroom ground-floor apartment with a little backyard. But it's the first home I've had where the bin is hidden. It's just a $30 special from our local hardware store, but it's so nice not to live in a share house with wine bottles and pizza boxes stacked up in a corner. A hidden bin is pretty sweet.

When Duncan and I started looking for our first home, we had no idea what we wanted. We didn't have much money, but what we lacked in coin, we made up for in naivety.

We signed the contract and, after a lengthy settlement, got the keys. Social media led me to believe that there would be some sort of fanfare when the agent handed over the keys. I'd heard stories about agents leaving bottles of bubbly and boxes of chocolates (the good kind) inside the house as a little surprise. Our agent left the keys in a pre-used envelope in our letterbox.

We thought we would do a little renovating here and there. A new kitchen, new floors and a new paint job. What do you find when you rip out the kitchen and flooring in a small two-bedroom apartment? Nothing! Your house is essentially gutted. So Duncan and I got stuck in. We were both working full-time, so each night after work we would eat a quick takeaway meal on the raw concrete floor and then take to the kitchen with sledgehammers and pickaxes. Around midnight we would pour ourselves into the car, drive the hour to my parents' house, shower, go to bed, get up and do it all again. It was one of the best times of my life.

We enlisted the help of a family friend to custom build our kitchen from scratch. Almost all the materials were salvaged from houses that were being demolished and we purchased a few items from a dump. The cupboards and drawers don't match, but somehow it works.

Everywhere I look in our home, there is a little piece of us or someone we love. You never know, the treasures you will (hopefully) make in this chapter may find themselves decorating the homes of the people YOU love.

Rope Vessel

You will need:

> 10 m (32 ft 9 in) of cotton rope

> 1 m (3 ft 3 in) x 1 m (3 ft 3 in) piece of paper to paint on

> Small craft paintbrush

> Water-based acrylic paint in your favourite colours

> Sewing machine with a zigzag stitch

> Sharp scissors

> Thread

Every living space needs a clutter catcher. Whether it's jewellery or guest soaps or potatoes, this beautiful rope vessel will keep all your bits and bobs neat and tidy. When your phone vibrates and you receive a message that your guests are 10 minutes away, quickly grab all those loose bits of household crap and throw them into a stylish handmade rope vessel. Suddenly your space will be transformed from scrappy to SNAPPY (OMG, LOL, did I just write that? – YOU BETCHA I DID!).

Rope Vessel

Step 1

Untangle the rope and place it on the large piece of paper. Using the acrylic paints, dab blobs of colour in random spots on your rope. Let your freak flag fly. This step is optional, so you can be as reserved or as colourful as you like. Allow to dry.

Step 2

Take one end of the decorated rope and coil it into a small circle, leaving a tail of loose rope. It should resemble the number 9.

Step 3

Once you have a coil that's big enough to sew, place it under your needle and slowly start to zigzag stitch the rope together. Bind the coil together by reversing over your stitches a few times to secure them. Repeat in the diagonal direction to the first line of stitching.

**Run out of rope?
Add another length of
rope by stitching the
ends together.**

Step 4

Once the coil is secure, slowly
begin to zigzag stitch the
loose rope to the coil. Be
sure that the zigzag stitch
captures the loose rope and
the coil as you sew. This will
be your vessel base.

Step 5

Continue sewing
the base until it
measures 14 cm (5½ in)
in diameter.

Step 6

As you continue to sew, lift
the base of the vessel and
hold it at an angle against
the left side of the sewing
machine. You will notice the
base begin to curve, giving
the vessel its sides. Continue
to sew until the vessel
reaches your desired shape
and size (about 8–10 cm
(3¼–4 in) high).

Step 7

Fold the last few centimetres of
rope underneath itself and sew
it down to finish. Alternatively you
can dip the end in paint to keep
it from fraying, but I like the little
folded-over nubbin.

*Keep the rope unravelled
and loose in your lap so
your machine doesn't
have to pull it up from
the floor.*

Not feeling up to getting out the paint and brushes? Did you know that blackboard contact paper is a thing? Simply cut out labels from the paper and apply them to your jars.

When we renovated our kitchen, I pored over lifestyle magazines and blogs, coveting their glistening kitchens with their beautiful exposed shelves. Nothing exposes your blocked digestive tract more than your entire kitchen pantry's contents displayed for everyone to see. So, I recommend a closed cabinet to store (hide) your instant noodles and beautiful, delicious, soft, sugary, white processed bread.

But your artisanal legumes?
PUT THOSE OUT ON DISPLAY!

Blackboard Labels for Dry Goods Jars

You will need:

› Many clean assorted jars in various sizes

› Wide paintbrush

› Blackboard paint

› Chalk or chalk pen

Step 1

Ensure your jars are clean and free from oil and dirt, both inside and out.

Step 2

Take the wide paintbrush and dip it into the blackboard paint. Using smooth strokes, paint a small rectangle on the front of each jar – approximately 7 cm (2¾ in) by 3 cm (1¼ in), depending on the jar size. Allow each to dry.

Step 3

Fill your jars and use chalk or a chalk pen to add labels. Display with pride and know that you will never, ever get close to finishing that enormous jar of dried barley pearls. But your friends don't need to know that.

Simple Macramé Plant Hanger

You will need:

› 20 m (65 ft 7 in) of cotton rope

› 1 metal ring measuring
  5 cm (2 in) in diameter

› 2 x 50 cm (1 ft 8 in) pieces
  of contrasting rope for
  the gathering wraps
  (see page 004)

› Scissors

› Measuring tape

› Embroidery thread in your
  favourite colours

› Super glue

› Water-based acrylic paint in
  your favourite colours

› Your favourite medium-
  sized plant

Bring the outdoors in by popping your favourite house plants into this decorative plant hanger. Plants take up a lot of room, so to avoid ground-level clutter, get some of those plants off the ground and up in the air!

What's stopping you from repurposing this project as a cool way to display a bouquet of flowers? Nothing!

Simple Macramé Plant Hanger

Step 1

Take the longest piece of rope and fold it so you are holding eight strands of equal length. Take the ring and thread it through into the middle. Fold the rope at the ring. You should now have 16 strands of rope hanging from it.

Step 2

Gather the strands of rope (near the ring) and, with one of the short pieces of rope, secure the 16 strands together using a gathering wrap (see page 004). Cut and separate the 16 strands at the other end.

Step 3

Measuring 20 cm (8 in) from the top of the ring, take four strands and tie four square knots (see page 003). Repeat this step with the neighbouring four strands until you have sets of four square knot clusters.

Step 4

Measuring 20 cm (8 in) from the bottom of your square knots, take a middle strand, along with an outer strand of one set, and marry it with a middle strand and an outer strand of a neighbouring set. Tie seven half knot sinnets (see page 003). Repeat until you have four sets.

Step 5

Measuring 15 cm (6 in) from the bottom of the half knot sinnets, take the middle strand, along with an outer strand of one set, and marry it with a middle strand and an outer strand of a neighbouring set. Tie two square knots. Repeat until you have four sets.

Step 6

Measuring 10 cm (4 in) from the bottom of the last set of square knots, gather all strands and, with the remaing short rope, use a gathering wrap to tie them together.

Step 8

I've never been one for cutting off loose threads and making everything symmetrical; however, you may like to take scissors and tidy up a few loose ends. To prevent fraying, dip the loose end of each rope strand into some coloured paint.

Step 9

Wait until the paint is dry, then position your favourite plant in the macramé hanger.

Step 7

Your plant holder is now almost complete. It is time to start embellishing. This is the fun part. Select some random strands of your plant holder and wrap the embroidery thread around and around to cover small sections. Fasten in place with a little dot of super glue.

After years of tending to leafy family members, I have curated a list of seven indoor plants that anyone can keep alive. If you are low on floor space, hang one up in a Simple Macramé Plant Hanger.

Heart Leaf Philodendron

I often forget to water this guy, even in some of my laziest months, and he is still going strong. Pop him near a window and water once a week. That's it.

Peace Lily

A classic bathroom plant. If you forget to water the peace lily she won't flower, but she will spring back. It takes a lot of effort to kill her.

Zanzibar Gem

To be completely honest, I forgot I owned this plant. I've watered her once in eight months.

Jade Plant & Other Succulents

Under the cover of darkness, snooping about my street, I can be seen swiftly taking cuttings of this plant from the gardens of my elderly Italian neighbours. This plant will grow in a simple jar of water or planted in damp soil.

Devil's Ivy

Another absolute gem, which will grow in a jar or in damp soil. Pop her next to a bright window and wait for her vines to get all dangly.

Echinopsis Oxygona & Other Cacti

I like my cacti big and dangerous! Our daughter is getting increasingly curious, so these types of house decorations have slowly moved upwards and out of reach. A cup of water once a month is enough to keep this guy out of trouble.

Monstera Deliciosa

This has to be my favourite plant. She is so unpredictable in the way she grows. Pop her near a bright window and feed her once a week. She grows upwards, sideways and is a little top heavy, so she may need support.

Rope C

◇◇◇◇◇◇◇◇◇◇◇◇◇◇◇◇◇◇◇◇

You will need:

> 10 m (32 ft 9 in) of cott

> Sewing machine with
> a zigzag stitch

> Sharp scissors

> Thread

> Warm water

> Indigo fabric dye

> Large bucket or bow

> Sewing needle

> A lamp missing its l
> (your local thrift sho
> have lots!)

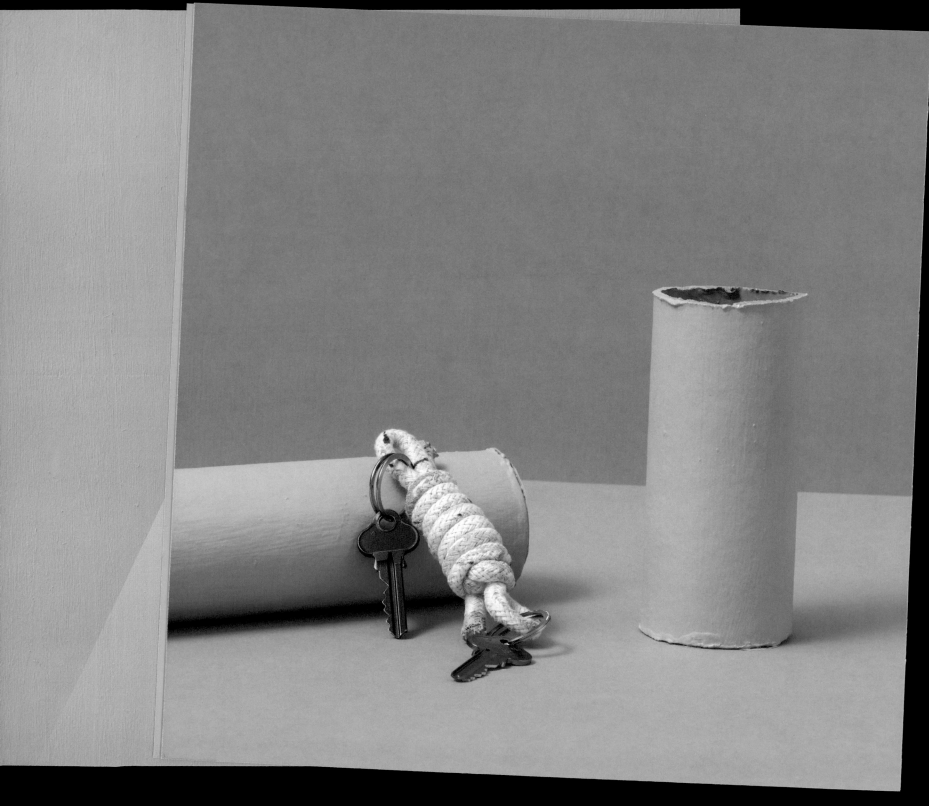

Double-sided Keychain

You will need:

› 1 m (3 ft 3 in) of cotton rope

› 1 m (3 ft 3 in) x 1 m (3 ft 3 in) piece of paper to paint on

› Water-based acrylic paint in your favourite colours

› Small craft paintbrush

› Scissors

› Measuring tape

› Super glue

› 2 standard keyring hoops

What is your mantra when you leave the house? Mine is PHONE, KEYS, WALLET! PHONE, KEYS, WALLET. My pal Dion will chant, 'spectacles, testicles, wallet and watch'. Three of those four items don't apply to me.

With every birthday brings a stack of keys. More responsibilities. I am in my mid-30s now, and man, I have a lot of keys/responsibilities. So it's time I streamlined my dungeon master key set: house keys on one side, and my studio and friends' spare keys (hello Jonny and Charlotte) on the other side.

Step 1

Take the rope and place it over the large piece of paper. Using the acrylic paints, dab blobs of colour in random spots on your rope. Leave to dry for a few hours.

Step 2

Once your rope is dry, cut a piece of rope measuring 25 cm (10 in). Glue the two ends of the rope together using the super glue. This section of rope should now resemble a circle.

Step 3

Pinch your circle rope together. Take the remaining section of rope and using a gathering wrap (see page 004), coil the rope around the middle of the circle rope. Leave 2 cm (¾ in) on either end. This is where the keys will hang from.

Step 4

Thread one keyring hoop through the open loop on each end. Tidy any loose ends of rope with the scissors and then dip the raw ends of rope into some acrylic paint to prevent fraying. Leave to dry. Once dry, spend a quiet moment organising your responsibilities.

Create an Impression

Everyone loves entertaining. Why is entertaining so … entertaining? There is just something about greeting your visitors at the front door and letting the smell of spices and oils hit them square in the nose. 'Phwwwaaarr, what smells so good!?' they'll ask. 'Butter,' you'll say!

I know I may have mentioned this already, but our home is small. Our ground-floor two-bedroom one-bathroom apartment has JUST ONE entertaining zone. Our entertaining zone is our lounge room, which bleeds into our kitchen.

Space is at a premium in our house, so when Duncan and I were designing our kitchen, we decided we wanted a dining table but didn't want to compromise the sense of openness. So we opted for a hidden dining table.

What the heck is a hidden dining table? Glad you asked. Have you ever gone caravanning with your grandparents? I have. It's like a cubbyhouse on wheels and there is hidden storage everywhere. Everything in that caravan was an illusion. I loved how the ironing board folded down from the back of the wardrobe, but my favourite thing was how you could fold the caravan table down level with the inbuilt bench seats, and through the magical rearrangement of cushions, you could make a second double bed.

Well, that was the inspiration behind our dining table! When guests arrive for dinner, we pull a section of our kitchen bench away from the wall to reveal a dinner table that comfortably seats six. It's just one of our #entertaininginasmallapartmentlifehacks.

There are lots of ways to ensure a memorable get-together, even if you don't have a lot of space.

In this chapter I will show you how to add a large serving of personality to your lunch or dinner party by offering your friends an experience as well as a tasty meal. Leave a great impression by adding personal handmade touches like placemats and napkin ring holders, or simply wow them with a refreshing cocktail.

Speckled Rope Napkin Rings

You will need:

› 30 cm (1 ft) x 3 cm (1¼ in) cardboard tube

› Sharp scissors

› 20 m (65 ft 7 in) of cotton rope

› Super glue

› Water-based acrylic paint in your 3 favourite colours

› Standard craft paintbrush

› 1 m (3 ft 3 in) x 1 m (3 ft 3 in) piece of paper to paint on

On those rare occasions when I use napkins, it's nice to dress them up a little. When I was younger, my family used napkin rings aaaaallll the time. At Christmas we would have to polish the special occasion silver napkin rings before carefully placing them back in the drawer to tarnish over another 364 days before we used them again. Whatever happened to fancy napkin holders? Let's bring back the napkin ring!

The great thing about these napkin rings is that you can refresh them on a whim. Simply get out your paints and change away!

Step 1

Take your tube and cut it into six individual tubes of equal length. These will be the bases of your napkin rings. Each napkin ring should measure approximately 5 cm (2 in).

Step 3

Coat your napkin rings with acrylic paint and leave to dry overnight.

Step 2

Untangle your rope and cut it into six equal lengths. Take a piece of rope, securing it at one end with a dab of super glue and wind it around one of the tubes from one end to the other. Once the cardboard tube is covered in rope, dab a little more super glue on the end of the rope, then fold and hide it underneath the other strands. Repeat this step until you have covered all six cardboard tubes with rope.

Step 4

Once the base coat is dry, decorate your napkin rings with speckles by flicking contrasting coloured paint over them from a height. Be careful – this step can lead to painted walls and clothes. Leave to dry for a few hours. Tuck some napkins into the holders and get ready for some awestruck guests.

Rope Placemats

You will need:

› 50 m (164 ft) of cotton rope

› 1 m (3 ft 3 in) x 1 m (3 ft 3 in) piece of paper to paint on

› Small craft paintbrush

› Water-based acrylic paint in your favourite colours

› Sharp scissors

› Measuring tape

› Sewing machine with a zigzag stitch

› Thread

Handmade rope placemats will add a wonderful personal touch to your next dinner party, but remember that they're destined to get dirty. I have used water-based acrylic paint from the hardware store so they can be machine-washed easily. If you want to add some flash to your placemats, ensure that your decoration can withstand a good scrubbing.

Step 1

Untangle the rope and place it on the large piece of paper. Using the acrylic paints, dab blobs of colour in random spots on your rope. Allow to dry.

Step 2

Untangle your decorated rope and cut it into six equal lengths measuring approximately 8 m (26 ft) each.

Step 3

Take one of your pieces of rope and coil one end into a small circle. It should resemble the number 9 with a small coil and a tail of loose rope. You should be a pro at this step by now!

Step 4

Place your coil under your needle and slowly start to zigzag stitch the rope together. Bind the coil together by reversing over your stitches a few times to secure them. Repeat in the diagonal direction to the first line of stitching.

Step 5

Continue sewing your placemat until it measures 25 cm (10 in) in diameter. Loop the last few centimetres of rope underneath itself and sew it closed, leaving a little nubbin.

Repeat with the remaining pieces of rope until you have six placemats.

There are lots of ways to ensure a memorable get-together, regardless of whether you're entertaining in a mansion or a shoebox-sized apartment. Here are some sure-fire ways to impress your guests and throw a killer shindig.

Get Comfy in the Lounge

No dining table? No problem! Just throw some cushions on the floor in a lounge room, plug in an electric frying pan, pop it on your coffee table and host an okonomiyaki evening! Don't we look like we're having fun? We definitely are.

Flowers – Nature's Centrepieces

If you only have time for one thing, make sure it's flowers. They invite conversation, touch and smell. Even better: introduce the crafty genius that is the Fresh Flower Fruit Skewers (see page 057).

Play Some Tunes

Don't have time to make a music playlist? Get your guests to play DJ. We have a great selection of vinyl records, but the problem is they require flipping quite often. So the first person to arrive is usually delegated DJ. 'Luke, please choose a record, something fun!'

The Art of Conversation

Free-flowing conversation can be a hard one to master. My trick is to get straight to the nitty gritty. Instead of asking your guests 'How was your day?', you might like to ask 'What was the best thing about your day?' Go deep.

Free-range Guests

Let your guests run free and investigate your home. To add intrigue, play a cassette of rattling chains and groaning sounds from a closed-off room and tape a DO NOT ENTER sign on the door. Serve them up a leg of lamb and drop creepy compliments like 'you look good enough to eat'.

Roped In

Abstract Rope Coasters

You will need:

› 7.5 m (24 ft 7 in) of cotton rope

› Sharp scissors

› Measuring tape

› Sewing machine with a zigzag stitch

› Thread

› Water-based acrylic paint in your 3 favourite colours

› Standard craft paintbrush

› 1 m (3 ft 3 in) x 1 m (3 ft 3 in) piece of paper to paint on

Save your beautiful Danish wooden coffee table from unsightly stains with this short, snappy project. By now you should be almost a pro with the sewing machine. Coasters are a great way to use up any scraps of rope from other projects.

Step 1

Untangle your rope and cut it into 10 equal lengths measuring approximately 75 cm (2 ft 6 in) each.

Step 2

Take a piece of rope and coil one end into a small circle. It should resemble the number 9 with a small coil and a tail of loose rope.

Step 3

Place your coil under your needle and slowly start to zigzag stitch the rope together. Bind the coil together by reversing over your stitches a few times to secure them. Repeat in the diagonal direction to the first line of stitching.

Step 4

Once your coil is secure, slowly begin to zigzag stitch the loose rope to the coil. Be sure that the zigzag stitch captures the loose rope and the coil as you sew.

Step 5

Continue sewing until all but the last few centimetres of the rope has been sewn into the side of your coaster. Loop the last few centimetres of rope underneath itself and sew it closed, forming a little eyelet nubbin. Repeat steps 2 through 5 until you have a neat stack of 10 round coasters.

Step 6

Coat your coasters with acrylic paint and leave to dry overnight.

Step 7

Once the base coat is dry, decorate your coasters with acrylic paints.

Fancy Up Your Watermelon

One time I was teaching a workshop and a friend's mother was attending. Let's call her 'Michelle'. Being a legitimate teacher's pet, she offered to help me cut up some fruit for morning tea. Michelle watched as I was about to butcher a quarter of a watermelon when she showed me that if I ran the blade of the knife between the rind and the flesh and then cut the melon into slices, I could nudge them into a zigzag ... pure genius.

Watermelon, Ginger Beer, Mint and Rum Pitcher

You will need:

› ¼ watermelon

› 1 large pitcher

› Long wooden spoon

› 500 ml (17 fl oz/2 cups) of white rum

› 1 large handful of mint

› Rolling pin

› 3 limes

› 4 cups of ice cubes

› 750 ml (25½ fl oz/3 cups) of ginger beer

Step 1

Remove the rind from the watermelon and chop the flesh into 2 cm (¾ in) cubes. Take half of the watermelon, place it in the pitcher and crush it with the wooden spoon. Set the remaining watermelon aside.

Step 2

Pour the white rum into the crushed watermelon flesh and stir well with the wooden spoon.

Step 3

Wash the mint and crush it lightly with the rolling pin. With your hands, tear it into rough 1.5 cm (½ in) pieces and stir into the mixture.

Step 4

Wash the limes and chop them into quarters. Add the limes, ice and remaining watermelon into the pitcher and stir.

Step 5

Stir through the ginger beer, pour into glasses and start talking dangerous truths!

Fresh Flower Fruit Skewers

You will need:

› 10 fresh flowers

› Sharp scissors

› 10 wooden skewers

› 1 roll of green florist tape

› 1 punnet of blueberries, washed

› 1 punnet of strawberries, washed

› ¼ watermelon, chopped into bite-sized portions (where possible, leave the rind on)

There is nothing more disappointing than when a friend serves fruit as a dessert. Isn't it just the worst?! Fruit – GRRROOOAAAN!!! These fresh fruit skewers are great to serve straight from the fridge on a hot summer afternoon to accompany cheese and wine. But if you are inclined to serve these beautiful ladies up as dessert, for the love of all that is good, serve them with a block of good quality chocolate.

Step 3

Take the blunt end of a skewer and insert it into the hole you just made. Use some florist tape to tape the flower in place. Repeat with the remaining flowers.

Step 1

Take your flowers and clean off any unwanted foliage from the flower heads. Cut the stems, leaving just 1 cm (¾ in) of stem attached to each flower head.

Step 2

Take the sharp end of a skewer and gently thread it through the centre of a flower stem and into the head of the flower, then remove it. Repeat with the remaining flowers.

Want to prepare these ahead of time? Use fake flowers instead of fresh.

Step 4

Carefully thread the blueberries, strawberries and watermelon onto the skewers and store these little guys in the fridge for a few hours before serving.

Formal vs Informal Dining

Dinner Settings Anyone Can Master

Ever since I watched *Pretty Woman*, I've been intrigued about how to navigate a formal dinner setting. Sometimes your dinner party needs that little something else to tip it over the edge from fancy to FANCEEEH!! I rarely set a formal dinner table, but the few times I have it looked spectacular. So, for your ease of reference, here is how to dress your table formally and informally. If I don't inspire you to host fancy dinner parties, at least this guide will give you some context on how to operate heavy dining machinery.

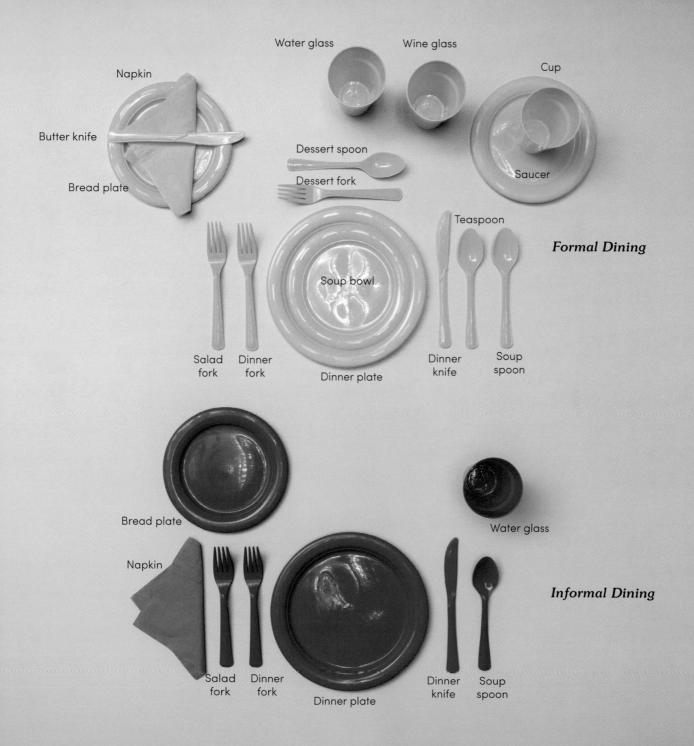

Ooh, Shiny

Where did you find those amazing earrings? I MADE THEM! *Drops mic*
OK, that scenario has never happened to me, but it's important to be prepared.

Sometimes I find my wardrobe lacks pizzazz. Let's be honest – I'm lucky if I even wear moisturiser most days! My priorities have shifted. My once leisurely routine of facial creams and bronzers has made way for nappy creams and rifling through the dirty laundry hamper for t-shirts that I can squeeze just one more wear out of. I'm the laundry carry-over champion.

Nowadays most of my outfits are either soft linen potato sacks or jeans worn with a stripey t-shirt. So, I thought I would include a chapter on items you can make and wear that drip with colour, texture and individuality.

Handmade fancy items maketh the most meaningful gifts. When you make something for a close friend, you get the opportunity to craft your friend's personality into the gift. That's pretty special. In this chapter, think about those nearest and dearest to you. What makes their style unique? Do they like busy, colourful fashion, or a clean, simple, pared-back style? Let your loved ones inspire you.

Friendship Knot
Earrings   p.069

'Diamond'
Necklace   p.073

Chunky Chain and
Rope Bracelet   p.075

Crafty Tip: Organising
Your Jewels   p.078

Swirly Rope
Jewellery Hanger p.080

Block
Blouse   p.084

Smocking   p.087

Itchy Fingers Easy
Embroidery   p.089

Friendship Knot Earrings

You will need:

> 40 cm (1 ft 4 in) of cotton rope

> Sharp scissors

> Embroidery thread in 2–3 complementary colours

> Some chain for some bling-a-ding

> Super glue

> Gold rope end caps

> Jewellery pliers

> 2 jump rings

> 2 earring hooks

One of my dearest friends recently married a handsome Austrian man, and instead of exchanging wedding rings, during the vows they bound their hands together with a ceremonial wedding knot. Isn't that beautiful? They literally TIED THE KNOT! I just think it is a lovely way of conveying love and togetherness. Tell your best friend you love them by crafting them a pair of friendship knot earrings.

Step 1

Take your rope and cut it in half. You should have two strands of rope measuring 20 cm (8 in).

Step 2

Think about your friend's favourite colours! Then take the embroidery thread of your choice and wrap it around sections of the rope. Tie off the ends of the embroidery thread and trim any loose bits with scissors. Be as creative as you like. Add some bling by threading some chain around the rope.

Step 3

Depending on how big you want your earrings to be, tie a loose knot and secure with extra embroidery thread. The top of the loose knot can also be bound together with a drop of super glue.

Step 4

Trim any excess rope and dab a little super glue on the raw ends of the rope. Insert the rope ends into the rope end caps. Using the pliers, thread the jump rings through the end caps and then carefully secure the earring hooks on the jump rings. Leave to dry for a few hours.

Making a pair for your best friend? Why not make a similar pair for yourself. Matchy matchy! #BUSTFRUNDS

'Diamond' Necklace

You will need:

› 7 m (23 ft) of cotton rope

› Sewing machine with a zigzag stitch

› Sharp scissors

› Thread

› Water-based acrylic paints in your choice of colour

› Wide paintbrush

› 1 m (3 ft 3 in) x 1 m (3 ft 3 in) piece of paper to paint on

› Super glue (a hot glue gun would also work)

› Large jewel stone

› Embroidery thread and needle

› 1 m (3 ft 3 in) of chunky chain

› Jewellery pliers

› 1 jump ring

› 1 jewellery clasp

When I say 'diamond' I really mean chintzy glass stone purchased from my local $2 shop, but that title didn't have the same va-va-voom. You can have a lot of fun with this design. You'll notice that this project is super simple. This is deliberate, and hopefully once you have mastered this initial design, you'll be inspired to make other shapes and styles.

Step 1

Take your cotton rope and coil it into a small circle. It should resemble the number 9 with a small coil and a tail of loose rope.

Step 2

Place your coil under your needle and slowly start to zigzag stitch the rope together. Bind the coil together by reversing over your stitches a few times to secure them. Repeat in the diagonal direction to the first line of stitching (see page 006).

Step 3

Once your coil is secure, slowly begin to zigzag stitch the loose rope to the coil. Be sure that the zigzag stitch captures the loose rope and the coil as you sew. Continue sewing until the coil measures approximately 14 cm (5½ in) in diameter.

Step 4

Cut your coil in half and coat both sides with a thick layer of acrylic paint. Set aside to dry.

Step 5

When dry, super-glue the large jewel into the centre of your painted semi-circle.

Step 6

Using the embroidery thread and needle, sew the chain into place around the semi-circle. Cut the chain to your preferred length.

Step 7

Using the pliers, thread the jump ring on to one end of the chain and then secure the jewellery clasp on the jump ring. It's ready to wear!

Chunky Chain and Rope Bracelet

You will need:

› 28 cm (11 in) of cotton rope

› 1 m (3 ft 3 in) x 1 m (3 ft 3 in) piece of paper to paint on

› Water-based acrylic paint in your favourite colours

› Small paintbrush

› Sharp scissors

› Super glue

› 2 gold rope end caps

› 2 jump rings

› Jewellery pliers

› 8 cm (3¼ in) of chunky chain

› 1 jewellery clasp

These simple yet fun bracelets are quick and easy to make. Just quietly, these are perfect (if you have the materials available) for those times when you're heading to a birthday party that day and you've forgotten to purchase a gift. Also, I don't mean to toot my own trumpet, but I was really happy with how these puppies turned out. This project is another great way to use up those fiddly strands of leftover rope from other projects. You'll never throw anything away again.

Chunky Chain and Rope Bracelet

Step 1

Take the rope and place it on a piece of paper. Splash some colour on it using the acrylic paints and a paintbrush. Leave to dry.

Step 2

Fold the rope in half, then cut it. You should have two strands of rope measuring 14 cm (5½ in). Dab a little super glue on the folded end and push it into the end cap. Repeat for the opposite ends. Leave to dry for 5 minutes.

Step 3

Thread a jump ring through each end cap.

Step 4

Using the pliers, fasten the chain on one jump ring, and the clasp on the other. Secure closed with the pliers and wear!

Jewel clutter is a sure-fire way to lose interest in accessorising. Don't worry! I've taken to the streets to ask Melbourne's most fashionable how they store their precious knick-knacks.

Danielle says 'do what the professionals do'

Head to a store that sells shop fittings and pick yourself up a necklace stand. The height of these stands can be adjusted and they're great to hang loads of necklaces on. Even better: make a Swirly Rope Jewellery Hanger (see page 080) to give your sparkles a swanky place to hang!

Amy suggests you 'organise your jewels by size'

Place little things with little things and big things with big things. You are less likely to lose the little delicate items when you're not mixing them with larger pieces.

Beck stresses that you should 'keep the bags they come in'

I find myself thinking, 'What can I use this for, a purse for ants?', but if you actually use them for their manufactured purpose (storing jewellery), your jewel clutter problem is solved.

Kath likes to 'hit the thrift stores'

Next time you are in your favourite second-hand store, scan the aisle for cute ceramics, which can double as ring dishes.

Dana insists you must 'always close the chain'

This little act of mindfulness will prevent dreaded tangles, unwanted loop-age and jewel weaving in your clutter catcher. I mean, it's so simple! A legit lightbulb moment. CLOSE THE CHAIN!

Ingrid recommends 'hot spot clutter catchers'

No-one knows your clutter habits like you do. My clutter zones are the bathroom, bedside table, kitchen sink and on top of the dresser drawers. Pop a little handmade rope vessel in these hot spots and catch that clutter!

Swirly Rope Jewellery Hanger

You will need:

› 15 m (49 ft) of cotton rope

› Sewing machine with a zigzag stitch

› Sharp scissors

› Pins

› 1 m (3 ft 3 in) x 1 m (3 ft 3 in) piece of paper to paint on

› Water-based acrylic paint in your favourite colours

› Small craft paintbrush

› Sharp, strong hand sewing needle

› Thread

This project is my version of jazz: freestyling on the sewing machine. It's 100% experimental and I hope it inspires you to create new shapes. This piece is really fun, but it's also a practical place to store your jewellery. When creating your project, remember to include some swirls and gaps to hang and thread your jewels through. Other than that, it has no rules. (Wait, I lied. There are some rules, but not many!)

Step 1

Untangle your rope and coil it into a small circle, leaving a tail of loose rope so it resembles the number 9.

Step 2

Once you have a coil of rope that's big enough to sew, place it under your needle and slowly start to zigzag stitch the rope together. Secure the rope coil in place by reversing over your stitches a few times. Repeat in the diagonal direction to the first line of stitching.

Step 3

Continue to add to the size of the rope coil by sewing the loose rope to the coil. Be sure that the zigzag stitch captures both the loose rope and the coil as you go. Once your coil measures 6 cm (2½ in) in diameter, remove it from the sewing machine, cut and set aside. Read Sewing a Rope Coil (page 006) for a refresher.

Step 4

Take another length of rope. Take one end of the rope and fold it (approximately 6 cm/2½ in lengthwise) onto itself. Using the same technique as in step 3, slowly begin to zigzag stitch the loose rope to the thin oblong-shaped coil. Continue sewing this oblong coil until it measures 9 cm (3½ in) in length. Remove the oblong coil from the sewing machine, cut and set aside.

Step 5

Repeat steps 3 and 4, but instead of 6 cm (2½ in) wide coils, sew coils at a few different sizes – some larger and some smaller. Get experimental. Create gaps by lifting the rope away from the coil and continuing to sew.

Step 6

Once you have sewn a collection of big and small shapes, arrange them in a nice shape on your work space. Pin them in place and use a zigzag stitch to carefully stitch all of the shapes together. Keep working on your swirly jewellery hanger until you have a shape you are happy with. The curvier and lumpier the better!

Step 7

Place your curvy, swirly hanger on the piece of paper and coat it in acrylic paint. Coat both sides and leave overnight to dry. Once it is dry, decorate! I drizzled paint directly over my hanger to give it a swirly look, but you may like to paint fun shapes. Find inspiration from your jewels! Set aside to dry.

Step 8

Using the sewing needle and some thread, sew a loop through the back of your hanger (you will have to push your sewing needle through the layers of dried paint, so push firmly). This is what you will use to attach your swirly hanger to the wall. Find a spot on your wall and hang your jewels in style.

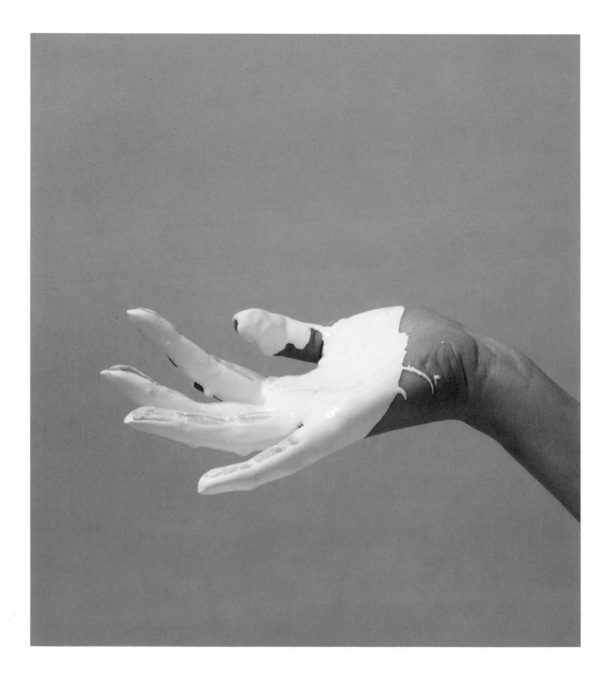

Block Blouse

You will need:

› 2 pieces of fabric measuring 1 m (3 ft 3 in) x 70 cm (2 ft 3 in)

› Sewing pins

› Sewing machine

› Matching thread

› Hot iron and ironing board

› Sharp scissors

› Measuring tape

What does 'right side' mean? Right side refers to the side of the fabric that faces outwards. The right side is the side that people can see when the project is finished, aka the side that collects food stains.

This is such an easy blouse pattern, you will make it again and again in different materials and colours. It's well worth the non-effort it takes to make and is a beautiful summer staple that will get lots of wear.

Step 1

Double hem all sides of the fabric by folding the raw edges of the fabric under itself. Pin, sew and press flat.

Step 2

Once all edges of your fabric are neatly hemmed, pin both fabric pieces together (right sides together). On one of the short edges of the fabric, mark the centre with a pin. Along the top, mark out the neck hole to measure 34 cm (1 ft 1 in) in the centre.

Step 3

Create the neck hole by sewing a straight line from the edge of the neck opening to the edge of the rectangle (or shoulder). Repeat on the opposite side.

Step 4

Create the sleeves by placing a pin 34 cm (1 ft 1 in) from the top of the shoulders on both sides. Sew the sides closed from the pin to the bottom hem.

You're done – yes, it's THAT simple!

You may notice that your blouse (while very pretty) is a stark blank canvas. Why not snazz it up with fabric dye? Or perhaps apply some of the techniques you will learn in the next two projects …

Smocking

You will need:

› 1 fabric square – size is up to you, but if you want to make a cushion, I would recommend your square is 70 cm (2 ft 3 in) x 70 cm (2 ft 3 in)

› Ruler

› 1 fabric pencil

› 1 medium sharp sewing needle

› 1 spool of matching thread

› Sharp scissors

I want to return smocking to those who are old enough to appreciate it. Those little bubbas who are swanning around in their beautiful hand-smocked dresses made out of pink and lavender imperial broadcloth have had it too good for too long.

There is a particular smocking technique that I love called 'flower smocking'. It's pretty easy and you know what ... I'll come clean. It's the only smocking technique I know. I'M A FRAUD!

Let me show you how to flower smock. You will never look at a scrap of fabric the same way again.

You can use this technique on pillows, blankets and throw rugs. Use it on anything. Everything!

Step 1

Lay your fabric square flat and neat on the table. Leaving a 2 cm (¾ in) seam allowance, starting at the top left corner, take your ruler and measure 2½ cm (1 in) on the right side of your fabric and mark it using your pencil. Repeat this step all over your fabric. Your fabric should be covered in evenly spaced dots and look somewhat like a grid.

Step 2

Concentrating on the first square (or set of four dots), take your needle and thread and make a stitch through dot 1, then dot 2, dot 3, dot 4 and finally dot 1 again so that you have created a square with the thread.

Step 3

Gradually pull the thread through nice and tight (without breaking the thread), bringing the fabric together so all the dots are drawn into the middle. Shape the petals with your fingers and secure with a double knot. It should now look like a flower with four petals. Repeat steps 2 and 3 until your fabric is covered in flowers.

Itchy Fingers Easy Embroidery

For me, embroidery is one of those classic couch crafts. The slow process of creating a personal artwork one stitch at a time really relaxes me. I recently fell in love with the craft while Duncan and I were on our honeymoon in the United States. Over six lazy weeks, we drove from New York to Los Angeles and in the middle states we saw some amazing applications of embroidery on jackets.

If you find yourself with a spare few hours up your sleeve, I strongly encourage you to pick up a needle and thread and try some of these basic stitches.

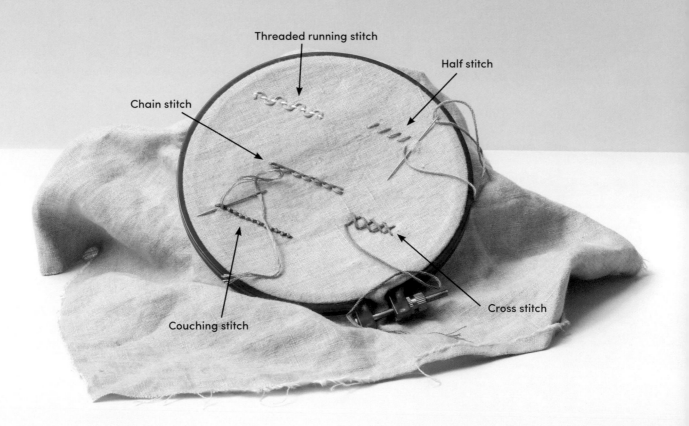

Threaded running stitch

Half stitch

Chain stitch

Couching stitch

Cross stitch

It Takes a Village

Duncan and I were so nervous when we brought our daughter Dusty home. We had no clue what-so-ever. We were pros in the hospital, but when it came to taking her home, I was so scared.

You should've seen us trying to put her into the car seat. I was convinced that we would break her while strapping her in. We immediately backed into a pole leaving the parking lot. We had 'new parents' tattooed onto our foreheads for sure.

What happened over the following weeks was miraculous. Our friends really rallied around us and carried us through the newborn fog. With Dusty came a huge sense of achievement. Strangers congratulated us and other parents told us what a wonderful job we were doing. Friends shopped for us, fed us, cleaned up after us and dropped care packages on our doorstep! It was wonderful.

Along with all the visits, Dusty won the lottery when it came to handmade gifts. Toys come and go, but as her room becomes overcrowded with baby items that break or are passed along to other families, all the handmade gifts she was gifted have remained. Some have been wrapped in tissue paper and stored away for the next baby or for her children. They are just too special.

This chapter offers ideas on handmade gifts you can create for those special little friends in your life and ways you can support those new parents navigating through scary, uncharted waters.

Self-binding
Baby Quilt p.097

Rope Alphabet
Letters p.100

Crafty Tip: What New Parents
Really Need p.102

Little Leg
Pantaloons p.104

Rope Planet
Mobile p.106

Self-binding Baby Quilt

You will need:

› 1 piece of linen fabric measuring 95 cm (3 ft 1 in) x 95 cm (3 ft 1 in)

› Thin paintbrush

› Water-based acrylic fabric paint in your favourite colour

› Sewing pins

› 1 piece of linen fabric measuring 115 cm (3 ft 9 in) x 115 cm (3 ft 9 in) in a complementary colour

› Sewing machine

› Thread of your choice

› Sharp scissors

› Hot iron and ironing board

Pretty much all of a baby's waking hours are either spent in their parents' arms, in a cot or pram, or on the floor. New parents don't vacuum, so a little quilt to throw on the floor to ensure the new little baby bird isn't rolling in cat hair is an ideal gift.

Step 1

Lay the smaller fabric square flat on your work surface. Take the paintbrush and paint your design on the fabric. Set aside to dry overnight.

Step 2

Take the small square of fabric and mark the exact middle of each side with pins. Take the larger square of fabric and, again, find the exact middle of each side. Again, mark each of these with a pin. Take your time with this, as accuracy is important.

Step 3

Place the two squares right sides together and pin the middles together on all four sides.

With the smaller square of fabric on top and starting from the middle, sew down the side of the square leaving a 1 cm (½ in) seam allowance. Repeat on all sides. However, on the last side, leave a 10 cm (4 in) opening, which you will use to turn the blanket right side out.

Step 5

Lay the blanket flat and press with a hot iron. You will see now how the larger square of fabric has folded over and is now the binding. Find the 10 cm (4 in) opening and ensure that the raw edges are folded neatly inside the blanket. Pin if necessary.

Step 6

With your blanket now neatly pressed, top stitch (I used a nice big zigzag stitch) along the fabric seams. Be careful when you come to the opening, as you want to ensure all the edges are sewn and hidden away.

Iron your finished blanket for maximum fanciness.

Step 4

Find the corner on all four sides and make a boxed (mitred) corner. This is tricky to explain, so stay with me ...

Take the blanket and lay it flat on your workbench. You will see that the corners have some extra fabric (I think they look like little ears). To mitre the corners, squarely fold the excess fabric on the side so it creates a little flat ear. Folding the fabric this way will create a natural straight line from the corner of the smaller piece of fabric to the outer edge of the large piece of fabric.

Stitch along this line and trim off the excess. Repeat this step on all corners.

Turn the blanket right side out.

Rope Alphabet Letters

You will need:

> 5 m (16 ft 4 in) of cotton rope per letter

> Sewing machine with a zigzag stitch

> Sharp scissors

> Pins

> 1 m (3 ft 3 in) x 1 m (3 ft 3 in) piece of paper to paint on

> Water-based acrylic paint in your favourite colours

> Small craft paintbrush

> Sharp, strong hand sewing needle

> Thread

Experiment with different letters. A lowercase B is similar to a lowercase A that has been flipped over with a longer tail. A lowercase C is a long, thin rope coil that has been curved around before sewing together.

With each day, Dusty picks up a new trick. I don't mean to liken her to an intelligent dog; it's more through parental 'training' that she picks up new sounds and words. 'Thank you' is 'dud-doh'. 'Dad' is also 'dud-doh'. Actually, she says her own name and that also is 'dud-doh', but each 'dud-doh' has its own inflection, and we are starting to communicate. This project is aimed to help toddlers learn letters through play. These letters are robust enough to play with, as well as being super cute to hang from a door or wall.

Step 1

Let's begin with the letter A in lowercase. Untangle your rope and coil it into a small circle, leaving a tail of loose rope. It should resemble the number 9.

Step 2

Place the coil under your needle and slowly start to zigzag stitch the rope together. Secure the rope coil in place by reversing over your stitches a few times. Repeat in a diagonal direction to the first line of stitching.

Step 3

Add to the size of the rope coil by sewing the loose rope to the coil. Be sure that the zigzag stitch captures both the loose rope and the coil as you sew. Continue sewing this coil until it measures 9 cm (3½ in) in diameter. Remove the coil from the sewing machine, cut and set aside. This will be the body of the letter A.

Step 4

Take another length of rope. Take one end of the rope and fold it (approximately 7 cm/2¾ in lengthwise) onto itself. Using the same technique in step 3, slowly begin to zigzag stitch the loose rope to the thin oblong-shaped coil. Continue sewing this oblong coil until it measures 10 cm (4 in) in length. Remove the oblong coil from the sewing machine, cut and set aside. This is the tail of the letter A.

Step 5

Arrange the body and tail of your letter A into a nice, recognisable shape on your work space. Pin it in place and using a zigzag stitch, carefully stitch the two shapes together. Hide away any loose ends of rope by sewing them into the joins of the shapes.

Step 6

Place your letter on the square of paper and coat it in thick acrylic paint. Set aside to dry.

Step 7

Using the sewing needle and some thread, sew a loop through the back of your letter (you will have to push your sewing needle through the layers of dried paint, so push firmly). This is what you will use to attach your letter to the wall. This step is optional.

The only thing that new parents really need is support: that's where you come in. Below is a useful list of things that really helped Duncan and me through the peaks and troughs of early parenthood.

I call this the 'sustenance with zero effort newborn care package' – food that you can prepare, heat and eat with one hand. It's nice knowing that at 3am, when you're nursing a newborn, there is always a tasty snack in the fridge!

› Casseroles, lasagne and curries in individual packets that can go straight from the freezer to the oven to the plate to the fork to the mouth.

› Breakfast jars (layer granola, yoghurt, chia seeds, frozen berries and honey in individual serving-sized jars).

› Fruit juice

› Fennel tea. It's said to help a nursing mother's milk supply. Neat stuff!

› Homemade granola bars

› Milk and a packet of biscuits (for visitor pop-ins)

› A block of good quality chocolate

› Fruit that can be eaten with one hand and requires no preparation – bananas, apples, berries

› Good-quality sliced bread

Sneak up to the front door and leave this lifesaving bundle of sustenance on their doorstep. Don't knock on the door or ring the doorbell as you may wake a baby they just rocked to sleep for 45 minutes. Instead, send them a text from the car and get the hell outta there!

Little Leg Pantaloons

You will need:

› Photocopier and paper

› 1 piece of jersey fabric measuring 1 m (3 ft 3 in) x 1 m (3 ft 3 in)

› Water-based acrylic fabric paint

› Pencil

› Sharp scissors

› Sewing pins

› Sewing machine

› Thread

› Hot iron and ironing board

› 1 m (3 ft 3 in) of thick elastic

› Large safety pin

You will be surprised and shocked by how many outfits a cute little cherub can CRAP THROUGH in one day. When you visit new parents, do their laundry and drop off a few pairs of these ...

Step 1

Photocopy the pattern provided (see page 164). Depending on the size of your new little friends, enlarge the image on a photocopier. The pattern provided is for newborns from zero to three months if cut to size.

Step 2

Lay the jersey fabric on the table. Using your finger, begin to paint fat polka dots on your fabric. Don't worry too much if your polka dots are not even in size. This will add to the handmade look. Leave to dry.

Step 3

Fold your fabric in half and lay the pattern on top of both layers. Carefully trace around the pattern and cut out the two pieces. The front and the back are the same pattern piece.

Step 4

Pin your little pants right sides facing each other and sew the fabric together along both sides.

Step 5

Once you have sewn the sides, sew the crotch together. Now flip the pants so they're the right side out.

Step 6

Hem the cuffs by folding the fabric 1 cm (½ in) inside the legs. Iron and pin down the hem so it sits well, and sew down using a wide zigzag stitch.

Step 7

Similar to the cuff, sew the waistband by double-folding the fabric 3.5 cm (1½ in) inside the waist. Iron down the waistband so it sits well. Sew it down, leaving a 3 cm (1¼ in) gap so you can thread the elastic through it.

Step 8

Cut a piece of elastic to size.

Attach a safety pin to one end of the elastic and thread it through the waistband. Remove the safety pin and then use the sewing machine to sew both ends of the elastic together. Sew the gap closed.

Step 9

Iron the pants flat. Aren't they cute?

While you have your fabric and machine out, consider making a few pairs. Little babies can go through four or more outfits a day!

Rope Planet Mobile

You will need:

› 20 m (65 ft 7 in) of cotton rope, plus extra for rope ring

› Sharp scissors

› Sewing machine with a zigzag stitch

› Thread

› Super glue

› Water-based acrylic paint in yellow, pink, blue, green, red, white and orange

› Small craft paintbrush

› 1 m (3 ft 3 in) x 1 m (3 ft 3 in) piece of paper to paint on

› Sewing needle

› Embroidery thread in your choice of complementary colours

I know I've mentioned this already, but babies do spend a lot of time staring at the ceiling. So why not give the baby something fun to look at? I have found that, from about eight months old, babies hate being changed on the changing table. They roll about and like to exercise their independence. This mobile offers a great distraction for speedy nappy changes.

Step 1

Take a piece of rope and coil it into a small circle. It should resemble the number 9 with a small coil and a tail of loose rope.

Step 2

Place your coil under your needle and slowly start to zigzag stitch the rope together. Bind the coil together by reversing over your stitches a few times to secure them. Repeat in the diagonal direction to the first line of stitching.

Step 3

Once your coil is secure, slowly begin to zigzag stitch the loose rope to the coil. Be sure that the zigzag stitch captures the loose rope and the coil as you sew.

Step 4

Continue to sew until your coil reaches your desired shape and size. Finish off your coil by looping the last few centimetres of rope underneath itself and sew it closed, leaving an eyelet. This is where you'll thread your string.

Sew nine rope coil circles. These coils will be your sun and planets. You may like to make them different sizes – i.e. the sun 15 cm (6 in), Jupiter 9 cm (3½ in), Saturn 8 cm (3¼ in), Uranus and Neptune 7 cm (2¾ in), Earth and Venus 6 cm (2½ in), Mars and Mercury 4 cm (1½ in). I know I know I know – these are not to scale!

Step 5

Take Saturn and super glue a rope 'ring' across the middle.

Step 6

Using the white acrylic paint, give all your planets a thick base coat. Set aside to dry.

Step 7

Using the water-based acrylic paints, decorate your coils to resemble your sun and planets. Set aside to dry.

Step 8

Once dry, fix your planets to the yellow coil – the sun – using a needle to get each embroidery thread through the painted rope.

Step 9

Take four lengths of embroidery thread, cut them to the same length and attach them roughly halfway out from the middle of the yellow coil, forming a square. Tie a strong knot at the top and hang.

The Furry Side of Life

Once, when Duncan was little, his family dog, Luke, ran away. After a lengthy time missing, he wandered home with a functioning dustbuster in his mouth. True story.

My brother had a little dog, aptly named Smidge. Smidge just adored my brother Brendan. Brendan adopted Smidge when he was living away from home for the first time. They shared a caravan and were pretty much best friends for life. Smidge was kicked by a horse when she was just a few months old and her little puppy leg was shattered. Brendan spent all his money (and man, he had none) on steroid treatments to keep the swelling in her leg under control. Her bed was heated and she was loved. WARNING – YOU'RE ABOUT TO CRY.

Smidge got really old and Brendan knew she was not well. Brendan got up to go to work one morning and Smidge, who was waiting for Brendan to wake, waddled over to him and quietly passed away. We humans have a strong connection with our furry friends. They are more than pets. They are members of the family. I am 100% convinced that our cat can say the word 'breakfast'. We say 'breakfast' and he echoes 'meep-marp'. There is something going on there. I know it.

Duncan, Dusty and I cohabitate our small apartment with a hefty ginger Garfield-esqe cat called Olly. Olly eats three small (calorie-controlled) meals a day and we are certain he flirts his way across our neighbourhood and eats a further 10 meals. At 4.30am each morning he starts scratching the back door and whining until we get out of bed to let him outside. Around 90% of the time Olly will decide he actually doesn't want to go outside, but rather look outside from the step of the open door. On the plus side, he lets Dusty pat him roughly and grab at his back fat. The peaks and troughs of pet ownership.

This chapter is dedicated to all our furry family members who scratch at the back door and can't decide if they want to be inside or outside or inside or outside or inside. If you make ONE THING from this chapter, please let it be the Caxedo. For the love of all that is good, please let it be the Caxedo! Because out pets deserve to be fancy too.

Swanky Dog Lead   p.115

Not-ugly Scratching Post   p.116

Crafty Tip: Cohabitating with Pets   p.118

Cat Tuxedo (Caxedo) Vest   p.120

Lazy Pooch Dalmation Print Dog Bed   p.123

Swanky Dog Lead

You will need:

› 20 m (65 ft 7 in) of cotton rope

› 1 m (3 ft 3 in) x 1 m (3 ft 3 in) piece of paper to paint on

› Water-based acrylic paint in your favourite colours

› Small craft paintbrush

› Swivel eye snap clip (medium size, or large enough for your rope to thread through)

› 1 m (3 ft 3 in) of extra rope for gathering wrap (see page 004)

This dog lead not only looks swanky, but it has a lot of elasticity, which means it won't pull sharply on your little pal's collar.

Step 1

Untangle your rope and place it over the large piece of paper. Using your acrylic paints, dab blobs of colour in random spots on your rope. Leave it to dry.

Step 2

Take your rope and fold it in half. Thread it through the swivel eye snap clip so that the clip is resting in the middle of the double strand of rope.

Step 3

Starting at the clip, tie a zillion half knot sinnets (see page 003). Notice how the knots form a beautiful spiral?

Step 4

Continue to tie half knot sinnets until your lead reaches the desired length. Leave a gap at the end large enough for you to thread your hand through and finish with a gathering wrap (see page 004).

Step 5

Dip any loose ends in acrylic paint and allow to dry. Now, strut your stuff at the park.

Consider making a matching collar for an extra bit of shmancy.

Not-ugly Scratching Post

You will need:

- 12 mm (½ in) plywood cut into a 40 cm (1 ft 3 in) diameter circle
- Strong PVA glue
- Cardboard mailing tube – measuring 9 cm (3½ in) wide x 45 cm (1 ft 5 in) long – with end caps. (You can cut the tube to length using sharp scissors)
- 3 small flat head screws
- Electric drill
- 40 m (131 ft) of cotton rope
- Sharp scissors
- Water-based acrylic paints in your choice of complementary colors
- Wide paintbrush

I've never met a scratching post I liked. Man, I know they serve a purpose and all, but most of the time they are soooo ugly. In this DIY project I will show you the fundamentals of making your own scratching post so you can craft and style it to your own personal space and taste!

Step 1

Find the centre of your plywood circle and glue one of the end caps onto it. Once you have glued the end cap into place, fasten it onto the plywood board using the three flat head screws and electric drill. This will be the base of your scratching post.

Step 2

Coat the edges of the end cap in glue and secure the cardboard tube onto the cap. Place some glue on the inner edges of the second end cap and fix it to the top of the tube.

Step 3

Unravel the rope. Starting at the base, carefully wind it around the plywood base and cardboard tube, gluing it down as you go. Once you reach the top of the tube, begin to work your way into the middle of the end cap. Cut away any excess rope and leave it to dry.

Step 4

Coat your entire scratching post in a thick layer of acrylic paint. Painting the rope will ensure that your kitten-cat doesn't tear apart your scratching post after the first scratch. Once your base coat is touch dry, give the scratching post some colour by painting it with your other paints.

Don't have room for a cat scratching post? Why not consider making one leg of your dining table or dining chair a scratching post. Simply gather-wrap some good quality rope around the leg of your chair or table. This will save your furniture and give your furry family member some instinctive release. Ahhhhhhhhhhh!

Our cat doesn't understand personal space. Where we are, he is.

If we are on the computer, he is trying to sit on the keyboard. If we are cooking, he is rubbing himself on our legs. The only person he gives A LOT of space to is Dusty. Dusty doesn't have the dexterity yet to pat Olly with the tenderness he is accustomed to. So, here's my advice to those living in small spaces and thinking about getting a pet ...

Go Ahead and Do It

I wouldn't recommend sharing your small space with a horse, but small, slow, affectionate pets work well!

Do Some Research and Know Your Breed

When you adopt your pet, speak to the staff. Tell them your living arrangements. Let the experts guide you. You want to avoid adopting a furry roommate who will destroy your home. This leads me to the next point ...

A Bored Dog is a Destructive Dog

If you have a jittery pet living in the confines of a small apartment, make sure you have the means to entertain her. Get her out into the big wide world for a walk and a good look around every day. She'll thank you for it, your furniture will thank you for it, and your backyard will thank you for it.

Keep Their Nails in Check

Cats are lovely creatures but HOLY CRAP – can it hurt when they affectionately paw at your knees. It was only recently that I learned that I should be carefully trimming Olly's nails. It is recommended that you gently trim or file your cat's nails once a month. Please be careful, and only trim off 1 mm. Just the very tip! Cat claws contain a lot of nerves and you don't want to hurt them.

Embrace Their Animal Instincts

Cats want to scratch and dogs want to run. Give your pets the opportunity to release their primal urges (that sounds gross) so they won't be tempted to do it on your furniture or in your shoes. This chapter shows you how to make a super stylin' scratching post (see page 116) and/or a swanky-looking dog lead (see page 115). Let your pets do what comes naturally.

Have Fun With Them

Pet cohabitation is the best. Kiss them, hug them, show them affection and when they wake you up at 3am, let your revenge manifest itself in the form of a Caxedo vest (see page 120).

Cat Tuxedo (Caxedo) Vest

You will need:

› Tape measure

› Photocopier and paper to enlarge or reduce pattern

› Sharp scissors

› Sewing pins

› 50 cm (1 ft 8 in) of cotton fabric in your choice of colour for jacket

› 50 cm (1 ft 8 in) of cotton fabric in a complementary colour for bow tie and shirt front

› Sewing machine

› Thread

› Hot iron and ironing board

› 1 medium sharp sewing needle

› Buttons

› Fake flower

› 20 cm (8 in) of Velcro

It's a sad state of affairs when your pet has a fancier wardrobe than you! Oh well. Count your blessings – you have opposable thumbs and can open jars.

Step 1

Get yourself invited to a fancy party where pets are welcome. This step is probably the most important, or you run the risk of sitting at home, cracking open a bottle of wine and hanging out with a pet who is better dressed than you.

Step 2

Measure your cat's neck and waist. Using a photocopier, enlarge or reduce the size of the pattern (see page 163) to your pet's measurements. Be sure to allow a few extra centimetres for the seam allowance.

Step 3

Cut out the pattern and pin it to your fabric. Once the pattern is fixed to the fabric with pins, carefully cut out the pattern pieces.

Step 4

With the right sides facing each other, sew the vest pieces together. Remember to leave a gap so you can turn the vest right side out.

Step 5

Turn out the vest, iron flat and sew the gap closed. Using a neat stitch, sew the shirt front onto the vest. Sew on the buttons and flower embellishment. It should now start to resemble a fun tuxedo!

Step 6

Cut a few centimetres of Velcro and sew the Velcro to the ends of the tuxedo waistband and the collar.

Step 7

With the right sides facing each other, pin and sew together the bow tie pieces. Again, leave a gap so you can turn the bow tie right side out. Turn the bow right side out, pinch it in the middle and wrap the small rectangular piece of fabric around the centre. Hand-sew the ends of the rectangular centrepiece of fabric together, ensuring the sewing at the back is not visible at the front.

Step 8

Hand-sew the bow tie to the collar and carefully dress your cat. Fix yourself a dry martini!

Lazy Pooch Dalmatian Print Dog Bed

You will need:

› 1 piece of dark grey cotton fabric measuring 2 m (6 ft 6 in) x 2 m (6 ft 6 in)

› Sharp scissors

› Measuring tape

› Pink fabric paint

› Sewing pins

› Sewing machine

› Dark grey thread

› Hot iron and ironing board

› 2 kg (4 lb 6 oz) of plush toy stuffing

› 1 medium sharp sewing needle

You know summer is underway when you find pet hair in your morning coffee. Save your expensive bed linen from excessive pet hair and craft your pooch a bed of her own!

You can substitute the plush toy stuffing with clean rags if you wish.

Step 1

Take your fabric and cut out a long strip of fabric measuring 2 m (6 ft 6 in) x 12 cm (4¾ in) plus two large circles measuring 60 cm (2 ft) in diameter.

Step 2

Dip your index finger into the pink fabric paint and start creating your dalmatian print, using the full pad of your finger to make long dots, and your fingertip to create short dots. Set aside for a few hours to dry.

Step 3

With the right sides facing each other, pin and sew together the cushion pieces. Start by sewing one circle at a time to the strip. Remember to leave a gap when you sew on the second circle so you can turn the cushion right side out.

Step 4

Turn out the cushion and iron flat. Take the stuffing and pack your cushion. Once the cushion is nice and full, hand-sew the gap closed. When the stuffing settles, you may like to unpick these stitches to add more stuffing, then sew it up again.

Get Festive

As I write this, I am slowly recovering from an epic weekend where we celebrated the joint bachelorette party for two of my dearest friends. I feel broken physically (hangover), but emotionally I feel whole.

This year Duncan and I will attend five weddings and two engagement parties, and sit on the steering committee for three bachelor/bachelorette parties. So, with this amount of immediate experience, I feel I am primed to impart some advice, projects and tidbits for those with special people about to celebrate those very special occasions.

I love getting ready for the holidays just as much as I like planning other people's shindigs. Last year was the first time we celebrated Christmas at home as a family. Duncan, Dusty and I woke up on Christmas morning and, without any particular forethought or planning, started our own family Christmas tradition. It really cemented the fact that we were our own little unit. Our own family. We are very close to our parents and siblings, but this was the first year I realised we had climbed off the mothership and boarded our own smaller satellite spacecraft. We weren't Gemma and Duncan anymore. We were Gemma, Duncan and Dusty, the Patford Legges (the Plegges), a new family celebrating Christmas for the first time on their own.

In this chapter I will show you how you can add some personal flair to your celebrations – handmade invites, table centrepieces, painted ornaments to hang on your prettiest house plants, and glittery bon-bons. Each project has just the right amount of wiggle room for you to go rogue and improvise a little, dressing it up to match your own fancy vision.

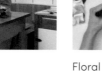

Pastel Rope Jar Centrepieces

You will need:

› 5 glass jars

› Assorted water-based acrylic paints in pastel colours

› Hot glue gun

› 20 m (65 ft 7 in) of cotton rope

› Wide paintbrush

Handmade elements are a great way to make your event unique. Consider decorating these easy centrepieces in a similar vein as your theme. If your theme is eggplants (aubergines), perhaps paint all your centrepieces in various shades of purple and green.

Fill your colourful centrepieces with bright, complementary colours or use white flowers for a bit of contrast.

Step 1

Take the jars and line them up in a row. Pour a blob of acrylic paint into the bottom of each jar and swish it around until the inside of your jar is completely covered in paint. Pour any excess paint back into your paint tin.

Set aside for a few hours to dry.

Step 2

Heat up your hot glue gun. Working from the bottom of your jar up, begin to coil and glue the rope to the base and side of the jar. Don't worry if you can see some of the glue – this will be covered up later. Coil the rope around the jar until it reaches the desired height. Snip off any excess rope, then tuck the loose end under and glue it down.

Step 3

Using a wide paintbrush, carefully paint the glued-on rope in a complementary colour. This may require two coats. Set aside to dry overnight.

Fill with flowers and cluster in the middle of your dining setting.

Ombré Pink Wedding Cake

You will need:

› 2 cakes*

› Sharp serrated bread knife

› Cake stand, board or large flat cake plate

› Flat spatula

› Icing

› 3 plastic drinking straws

› Red food colouring

› Sharp scissors

* For my Classic Wedding Cake Recipe, refer to page 161.

> *What's a crumb coat, you ask? Your crumb coat is a thin preliminary layer of icing that will keep any dark crumbs from making their way into your beautiful outer layer.*

Styling and decorating your cake seems a lot harder than it is. It's actually relatively simple. This is because I like to make my cakes rough, with icing I can accidently stick my finger into and no one will notice.

Step 1

Take the cakes and cut off the rounded cake tops to make them nice and even. On your cake stand, plate or board, add a blob of icing (this blob will fix the cake securely to the cake stand) and flip your cake upside down so that the bottom of the cake is now on top. This will make your cake top super flat.

Step 2

Smooth a thin layer of icing on – approximately 1 cm (½ in) thick – and place another cake on top. Remember to flip this cake upside down, too, so that the top of your cake is nice and flat.

My trick here is to insert some load-bearing straws into the cake. This will prevent the layers from shifting. Cut them to size and ice over the little holes they leave behind.

Once the cake is nice and tall, take a flat spatula and put an initial layer of icing, called a crumb coat, onto your cake. Place in the fridge for 30 minutes to set.

Step 3

Now it's time to get creative. Divide your icing into three separate bowls. Add three drops of red food colouring in one bowl, and add only one drop in another. Mix until the colour is consistent in each bowl. You should have one pink batch of icing, one light pink batch of icing and one white batch of icing.

Step 4

Using the spatula, apply a thick layer of the darkest pink icing around the bottom third of your cake. Once applied, move on to the lighter pink colour and apply a thick layer around the middle third. Next, take the white icing and apply a thick layer around the top third.

Step 5

Once all three layers have been iced, clean your spatula and, using its long flat edge, smooth out the icing and watch it blend nicely together into an ombré effect. There is no need to be too careful. The blended texture of the colours works well with a few lumps and bumps.

Floral Invitations

You will need:

› Assorted fake flowers

› Thick white card

› Sharp scissors

› Wide paintbrush

› Craft glue

› Good fineline pen

› A colour scanner/photocopier (head to your local library)

› Craft knife

I call stationery like this 'accrued value', as these handmade gems really manage to lift an occasion from casual meal to a fancy dinner.

The project I am about to share with you can be translated across a few different platforms. I love a theme – it's no lie – and flowers are the easiest theme in the world.

Step 1

Destroy the fake flowers – pull off all the petals and place them to one side.

Step 2

Using scissors, cut the white card to roughly the size of your invitation. Don't worry about making this exact, as you can trim this to size later with the craft knife.

Step 3

Paint a good thick layer of glue along the bottom third of your card. Starting from the top of the glue, carefully press a horizontal row of flower petals into the glue.

Once you have completed the first row, carefully press another horizontal row of flower petals into the glue just below. This row should just overlap the row above it.

Continue to press row after row of flower petals into the glue until the bottom third of your card is covered.

Step 4

You can always paint a good thick layer of glue along the top of the card (not pictured). With the flower petals facing upside down, carefully press a horizontal row of petals into the glue.

Set aside for 20 minutes to dry.

Step 5

Once the glue is touch-dry, grab your good black fineline pen. (Ohhhhhhkayyyyy – listen to me. You don't want to spend all this time hand-making fancy-as-hell invitations, only to ruin it here using a crappy blue ballpoint pen). Now, in your best handwriting, write the details of the invitation onto the card.

If you have a zillion people coming to dinner, or you are planning a wedding, you may want to scan and colour copy this original. This is an especially good idea if you want to replicate lots of invitations. Alternatively, you can scan the image into an editing program and type the details in using a fancy font. The scanned images look great as most scanners will pick up the slight shadows behind each petal and give the invitations a beautiful 3D feel.

Step 6

Trim to size with the craft knife.

If you're keen, menus

Following the steps for the invitation, craft up a beautiful menu. You may like to make a menu for each guest, or place one or two on each table.

If you're super keen, place settings

Assigned seating is a great way to get your guests mingling. If I'm hosting an intimate party, I like to make personalised place settings by taking a 10 cm (4 in) x 5 cm (2 in) strip of card and styling it in the same way as the menu. Then, using a sharp craft knife, I cut out each attendee's initials. It creates a very simple and clean design.

If you're really super keen, thank you cards

With every party comes guests – and good guests contribute, either with chocolates or a bottle of wine, or simply by bringing their conversational A-game. Good guests equals a good party. So, if you're super keen and want to send your partygoers some snail mail, send them an on-theme thank you card.

Soap on a Rope

No matter the gift occasion, my father would always joke that he wanted a soap-on-a-rope. So, I couldn't resist including a fun, tongue-in-cheek soap-on-a-rope project.

You will need:

› 40 cm (1 ft 3 in) of cotton rope
› Soap
› Electric drill

Step 1

Grab some paint-speckled rope left over from another project, or get out your paint and create some from scratch. Dip the ends in paint to seal them and leave to dry.

Step 2

Create a nice clean hole through the centre of your soap using the electric drill.

Step 3

Fold the rope in half and thread it through the hole in the soap. Tie a knot on either side of the soap and hang it from your shower.

Rope Tote

You will need:

> 30 m (98 ft 5 in) of cotton rope

> 1m (3 ft 3 in) x 1m (3 ft 3 in) square of paper to paint on

> Small craft paintbrush

> Measuring tape

> Sewing machine with a zigzag stitch

> Sharp scissors

> Thread

> Pins

> Water-based acrylic paint in your favourite colours

This rope tote is the perfect size for housing your packed lunch, phone, keys and purse. During the festive season, it's a great way to carry home your Christmas haul and itty bitty stocking stuffers. I love a gift you can sneak home leftover ham in, too!

Step 1

Untangle your rope. Take one end and fold it (approximately 12 cm/4¾ in lengthwise) onto itself.

Step 2

Place folded rope under your needle and slowly start to zigzag stitch the rope together. A thin oblong coil will begin to form. Continue to add to the size of the rope coil by sewing the loose rope to the coil. Be sure that the zigzag stitch captures both the loose rope and the coil as you sew.

Step 3

Continue sewing this coil until it measures 20 cm (8 in) in length and 12 cm (4¾ in) in width. This will be the base of your rope tote.

Lift the base and hold it at an angle against the left side of the sewing machine. Continue to sew more of the loose rope to the coil. You will notice that the rope will begin to curve and the sides of the rope tote will begin to form. Continue to sew the sides of the tote until it reaches about 17 cm (6¾ in) in height. Remove it from the sewing machine.

Step 4

Let's talk handles! If you refer to the image, I left a gap for my arm to fit through, which was 12 cm (4¾ in) wide. To accomplish this, I used pins to mark 6 cm (2½ in) on either side of the middle point along the top of the basket. With the pins in place, continue to sew your tote until you reach the first pin.

Step 5

Stay with me, this is about to get wordy. From the first pin, measure out 47 cm (18½ in) of loose rope. Attach another pin to the lose rope at the 47 cm (18½ in) mark, which will be where your handle ends. See, it is even starting to look like a handle! Line up the handle pin with the second pin on the basket.

Step 6

Beginning at the second pin, sew the handle to the basket. Sew the rope until you reach the next (third) pin. Repeating what you did on the other side, measure out 47 cm (18½ in) of loose rope. Attach a fourth, and last, pin at the 47 cm (18½ in) mark. Repeat these steps, sewing the rope until your handles are nice and thick. I recommend your handles are at least three ropes thick!

Step 7

Loop the last part of the rope underneath itself and sew it closed.

Step 8

Paint the bottom half of your tote and leave it to dry overnight.

Glitter End Bon-bons

You will need:

› A3 sheet of white cardboard

› Sharp scissors

› Ruler

› Double-sided tape

› 6 sheets of brown A4 paper

› Wide paintbrush

› Craft glue

› Assorted coloured glitter

› Little treasures

What is a holiday table without a bon-bon or cracker? These crackers are particularly great, as you can fill them with treats you actually want and to suit any type of celebration.

Ideas for treasures to pop in your bon-bons:

› *Terrible jokes – such a classic!*

› *Ice-breaker truth or dares*

› *Your favourite sweets*

› *Fake moustaches*

› *Poems*

› *Plant seeds*

Even if you have the space for a pine tree, sometimes it's nice to try something a little different – especially if that something comes with fewer pine needles digging into bare feet.

Work With What You've Got

Why not opt to decorate your existing house plants? Think about it. You already have a house full of beautiful plants just crying out to be covered in tinsel and some sweet rope ornaments. Choose your favourite and cover her in holiday cheer.

Fake It Until You Make It

You want a Christmas tree? You like Christmas trees? Well then honey, YOU GET YOURSELF A CHRISTMAS TREE! How about a poster of a Christmas tree? Get your camera out and head to your local town centre. Most cities have a beautiful festive tree display from October onwards. Take a good photo of the city-funded tree, print the photo on a poster and hang it on your wall. Not confident with the camera? There are some wonderful artist prints online. Clutter the bottom with gifts and you've got a two-dimensional tree!

NOPE to Tree

Want to circumvent the tree thing altogether? If you have an ornamental fireplace, make it your Christmas zone. If you hang enough stockings from the edge and fill the fireplace with gifts, no one will even notice it's not green and leafy.

Economy of Scale

Let's face it. You just want a tree and no amount of craftwork is going to stop you from wanting a real Christmas tree. So, get a tiny one. I'm talking the size of a shoebox. Most nurseries cater for #apartmentlyfe and sell teeny tiny trees. Embrace the cuteness and make teeny tiny ornaments, and wrap teeny tiny gifts. MINNY CHRISTMAS!

Rope Coil Christmas Bell Ornaments

You will need:

› 1 m (3 ft 3 in) of cotton rope

› Sewing machine with a zigzag stitch

› Sharp scissors

› Thread

› Wide paintbrush

› Water-based acrylic paint in your favourite colours

› 1 m (3 ft 3 in) x 1 m (3 ft 3 in) piece of paper to paint on

› Craft bell

› Strong embroidery needle

A fun little take on the classic rope vessel. This project literally turns the vessel on its head to create little bells for your Christmas tree.

Step 1

Take the rope and coil one end into a small circle. It should resemble the number 9 with a small coil and a tail of loose rope.

Step 2

Place your coil under your needle and slowly start to zigzag stitch the rope together. Bind the coil together by reversing over your stitches a few times to secure them.

Step 3

Once your coil is secure, slowly begin to zigzag stitch the loose rope to the coil. Be sure that the zigzag stitch captures the loose rope and the coil as you sew. This will be the top of your bell. Continue sewing the top of the bell until it measures 2–4 cm (¾–1½ in) in diameter.

Step 4

As you continue to sew, lift the coil and hold it at an angle against the left side of the sewing machine. Continue to sew. You will notice that the shape will curve, giving the bell its sides.

Step 5

Continue to sew until your bell reaches your desired shape and size. Loop the last few centimetres of rope underneath itself and sew it closed.

Step 6

Coat your bell with acrylic paint and leave to dry overnight.

Step 7

Secure the bell to the embroidery thread and use the needle to push it through the bell's centre. Tie a double knot on either side of the rope coil so the bell hangs where you want it. Trim the thread and knot it to form the hanger.

These little rope bells
make cute holiday gifts
for friends!

3D Gingerbread Centrepiece

Every time we would visit Nanny Patford, we would make a beeline for the corner cupboard, pull out an old tin and prise open the lid to find the ALADDIN'S CAVE of GINGERBREAD MEN. Her gingerbread men were always soft, chewy and spicy, and because she had a massive lemon tree dripping with fruit, they were always iced with a tangy lemon icing. I was a chubby child, and I can safely attribute the extra calories to this gingerbread recipe.

I've tried Nan's recipe and, despite my best efforts, I cannot get my gingerbread as good as hers. This leads me to think she took her true recipe to the grave. One last UP YOURS for making her bake a million odd gingerbread men (and for eating all the Fishermen's Friends from her purse). It's taken me years of trials, but I think I've now got a recipe that is almost (but not quite) as good as Nan's.

You will need:

› Baking tray
› Baking (parchment) paper
› Electric mixer
› Sifter
› Plastic wrap
› Photocopier or pencil and paper
› Rolling pin
› Sharp knife
› Wire rack
› Spatula

Gingerbread:

› 125 g (4½ oz) butter, softened
› 95 g (3¼ oz/½ cup) brown sugar
› 60 ml (2 fl oz/¼ cup) treacle
› 60 ml (2 fl oz/¼ cup) golden syrup or corn syrup
› 1 egg
› 50 g (⅓ cup) plain (all-purpose) flour
› 225 g (1½ cups) self-raising flour
› 2 tablespoons ground ginger

Icing:

› 1 large egg white
› 215 g (7½ oz/1¾ cups) icing (confectioners') sugar
› 1 teaspoon lemon juice

Step 1

Preheat your oven to 170°C (340°F). The lower heat will ensure the gingerbread cooks slower and remains chewy. Line a baking tray with baking paper.

Step 2

Using an electric mixer, beat the butter and the sugar together until pale and creamy (approximately 4 minutes). Slowly add the treacle, golden syrup and the egg. On a slower speed, gradually add the sifted dry ingredients until the mixture forms a dough.

Roll the dough into a ball, cover in plastic wrap and place in the fridge for 30 minutes. While the dough is chilling, photocopy or trace the Christmas tree template provided (see page 165).

Step 3

Once your dough is chilled, knead on a lightly floured surface, then roll the mixture out onto baking paper until it's approximately 1 cm (½ in) thick.

Step 4

Gently place the template over the dough and cut two Christmas tree shapes from your dough. Then cut one tree in half from top to bottom.

Step 5

Carefully transfer your tree shapes onto the lined baking tray. Bake for 10–15 minutes, or until golden brown around the edges. Place on a wire rack to cool.

Step 6

Make the icing. Using an electric mixer, beat the egg white for about 4 minutes until firm peaks form. Gradually add the sifted icing sugar and beat until fully combined. Add the lemon juice and beat for a further minute.

Step 7

Using the icing as glue, stick the two half gingerbread trees on a right angle to the large gingerbread tree. Set aside to dry.

Step 8

Once your tree is dry and stable, decorate as desired. I decorated these simply with the icing made in step 6. For a fancy touch, consider decorating with cachous balls. These trees make wonderful edible centrepieces, which can be enjoyed with coffee at the end of the meal.

Consider making some smaller gingerbread ornaments in the shape of bells, circles and little Christmas trees for your tree by poking a little hole through the biscuit using a toothpick and looping some string through.

Festive Wreath

You will need:

› 10 m (32 ft 9 in) of cotton rope

› Sharp scissors

› Kitchen string

› Wide paintbrush

› White water-based acrylic paint

› 1 m (3 ft 3 in) x 1 m (3 ft 3 in) piece of paper to paint on

› Assorted fake or fresh flowers

› Sewing awl

› 4–6 wool pom-poms

› 4–6 tassels

More is more. I'm the first to say it. However, each Christmas I find myself looking for a simpler, more pared-back way to spread festive cheer. This season I am searching for relaxed, livable, natural pieces to decorate our small apartment. Using fake flowers and neutral colours, this hand-painted, hand-braided wreath will look great in a variety of spaces.

Most craft stores stock a wonderful selection of pre-made pom-poms and tassels.

Step 1

Cut your rope into nine equal strands. Using kitchen string, tie them together at one end and braid together. In bundles of three braids, bend the rope into the shape of a horseshoe, and paint one side of your wreath white. Leave to dry for approximately 2 hours and then paint the other side. Leave to dry overnight.

Step 2

OK! Now that it's dry, let's start the fun stuff. Decorate your wreath. Take the flowers and clean them up a little bit if they're fresh. You want to be able to thread the stems through the gaps in the braid. How you decorate your wreath is completely up to you. I opted to focus on a small portion of my wreath to give it a more relaxed, pared-back vibe.

Step 3

Using your awl, you may need to pierce the wreath to thread your flower stems through. Create some texture into your wreath by muddling the pom-poms and tassels in among the flowers. You may wish to fasten your decorations using kitchen string. Don't panic if you can see the string – it simply adds to the handmade look.

Step 4

Once you're happy with it, hang this puppy on your front door and share some holiday cheer with your neighbours.

Classic Wedding Cake Recipe

One way you can score an invite to any wedding is to offer to bake their cake! So I haven't left you hanging with the ombré cake decorating project (see page 136), here is my tried and tested, classic special occasion cake recipe. It's simple and you can make it two weeks in advance.

You will need:

› 20 cm (8 in) baking tin

› Baking (parchment) paper

› Baking spray

› Sifter

› Skewer

› Electric mixer

White chocolate mud cake:

› 250 g (9 oz) good-quality butter

› 200 g (7 oz) good-quality white chocolate

› 460 g (1 lb/2 cups) caster (superfine) sugar

› 125 ml (4 fl oz/½ cup) boiling water

› 1 tablespoon glycerine

› 2 tablespoons good-quality brandy

› 150 g (5½ oz/1 cup) self-raising flour

› 150 g (5½ oz/1 cup) plain (all-purpose) flour

› 1 tablespoon custard powder

› 1 tablespoon cornflour (cornstarch)

› 3 eggs

Buttercream frosting:

› 400 g (14 oz) unsalted butter, at room temperature

› 1 teaspoon vanilla extract

› 60 ml (2 fl oz/¼ cup) milk

› 1 kg (2 lb 3 oz) pure icing (confectioners') sugar

Step 1

Line your baking tin with baking paper and cover generously with baking spray. Preheat your oven to 160°C (320°F).

Step 2

In a medium saucepan over low heat, melt and combine the butter, chocolate, sugar, boiling water, glycerine and brandy. Once the sugar has dissolved, set aside to cool.

This cake gets more dense and moist after one week. Wrap your cake in plastic wrap and store in your freezer for up to three weeks. If you want to make a nice, tall dessert, bake multiple cakes.

Step 3

In a separate bowl, sift together the self-raising flour, plain flour, custard powder and cornflour.

Step 4

Whisk three eggs into the chocolate mixture and gradually fold in the sifted flour mixture. Once combined, pour into your baking tin. Lightly tap the side of your tin to remove any air bubbles (this makes the cake beautiful and dense).

Step 5

Place the tin into the preheated oven for 1 hour. To test the cake, insert a skewer. If the skewer comes out clean, the cake is cooked through.

Step 6

Using an electric mixer, beat the butter and vanilla until it is pale and soft. Gradually add the milk and icing sugar alternately (add a cup of sugar then a splash of milk), until the frosting is smooth and white. Depending on the size of your cake, you may need to make multiple batches.

Patterns

These patterns are designed to be scanned and adjusted to whatever size you need them to be. I can't imagine that many readers have a cat as large as my Olly, but you never know.

Cat Tuxedo (Caxedo) Vest

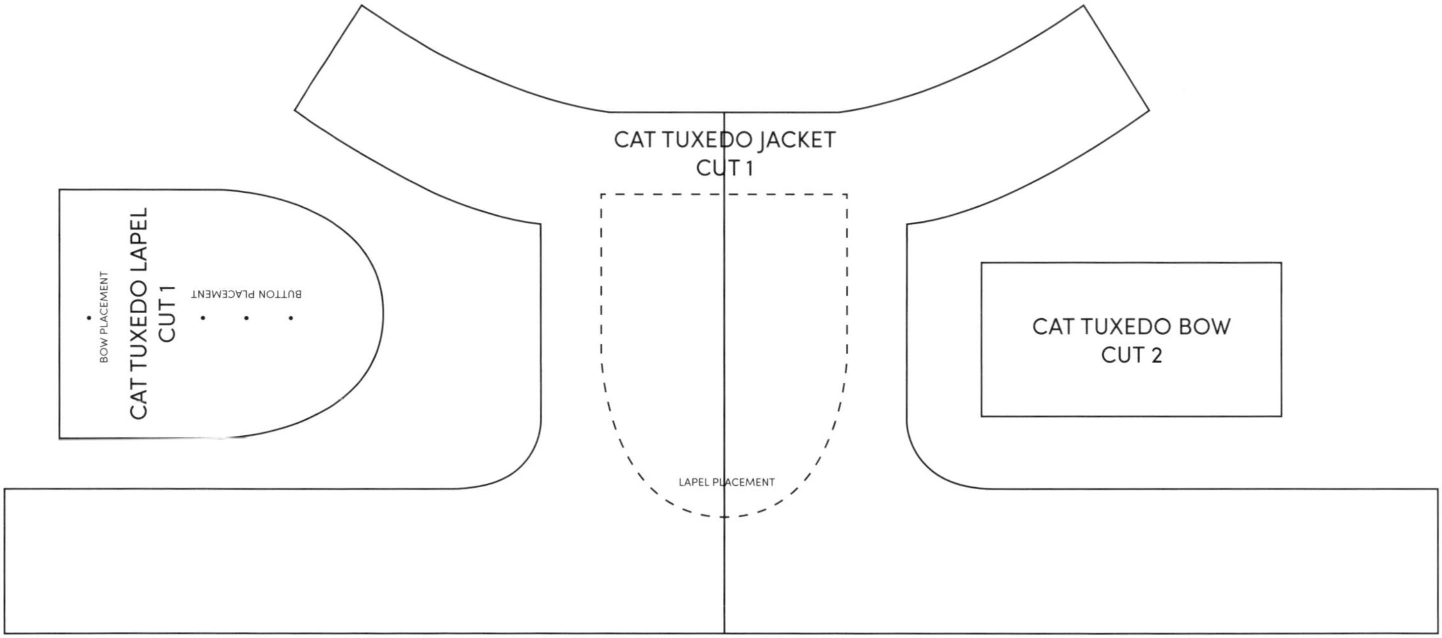

CAT TUXEDO JACKET
CUT 1

LAPEL PLACEMENT

CAT TUXEDO LAPEL
CUT 1

BOW PLACEMENT

BUTTON PLACEMENT

CAT TUXEDO BOW
CUT 2

Thank You

I would really really really like to thank the following legends ...

Duncan and Dusty for keeping me inspired and lighting fires under my seat.

My main ladies, Jessica Blume and Robyn Clark. Without these women, GemmaPatford.com would not exist.

To my talented, nimble, hilarious group of volunteers: Amelie Inard, Kashia Kennedy, Marianne Duval, Gabrielle Devlin, Adrienne Aiple-Nigli, Susi Matovski, Amy Devereux, Anthea Abell and Nicola Camporeale.

The Design Files for giving me such an amazing start.

Jonny Lucy for injecting spice into my writing.

Jess and Lara from Home-Work for talking me back from the ledge (every day) and opening up their beautiful work space and hearts.

The team at Hardie Grant Publishing for laughing at my lame jokes and pushing my ideas into reality.

Monash HR for always supporting my extra-curricular activities.

Danielle, Ingrid, Dana, Jess, Kath, Amy, Beck and Sarah for unwavering support and encouragement, even in the face of ugly craft and terrible ideas.

My sister Belinda for baby wrangling and being my biggest PR agent.

My brother Brendan for sharing his woodworking expertise.

To everyone who has ever made contact asking me to share ideas, methods, tips and tricks! This book is your brainchild!

Most importantly, Mum and Dad for always having an open paint tin and a role of masking tape available.

Beautiful people and products featured in this book:

Shoes by Radical Yes

Linen by Mr Draper

Flowers by Cecilia Fox

Pink sports bag by Witu

Hand-crafted soap by Twig & Clay

Delicate hand models Adrienne Aiple-Nigli, Kate Armstrong and Sally Addinsall

Obedient pooch Bo Addinsall

Dash and spot mug by Leah Jackson

Coloured paper backgrounds by K W Doggett – The Paper People

Published in 2017 by Hardie Grant Books, an imprint of
Hardie Grant Publishing

Hardie Grant Books (Melbourne)
Building 1, 658 Church Street
Richmond, Victoria 3121
hardiegrantbooks.com.au

Hardie Grant Books (London)
5th & 6th Floors
52–54 Southwark Street
London SE1 1UN
hardiegrantbooks.co.uk

A Cataloguing-in-Publication entry is available from
the catalogue of the National Library of Australia at
www.nla.gov.au

Roped In
ISBN 9781741175257

Commissioning editor: Melissa Kayser
Managing editor: Marg Bowman
Project editor: Kate J Armstrong
Editor: Susie Ashworth
Proofreader: Eugenie Baulch
Design manager: Mark Campbell
Designer: Vaughan Mossop
Typesetter & pre-press: Megan Ellis
Photographers: Jessica Reftel Evans & Martin Reftel (Amorfo)
Stylist: Gemma Patford
Illustrators: Ashley Ronning, Gemma Patford
Production manager: Todd Rechner

Colour reproduction by Splitting Image Colour Studio
Printed in China by 1010 Printing International Limited